Health Zone

STAY fit!

How YOU Can GET IN SHAPE

Matt Doeden

illustrations by Jack Desrocher

Consultant: Sonja Green, MD

Lerner Publications Company
Minneapolis

All characters in this book are fictional and are not based on actual persons. The characters' stories are not based on actual events. Any similarities thereof are purely coincidental.

Lerner Publications Company
A division of Lerner Publishing Group, Inc.
241 First Avenue North
Minneapolis, MN 55401 U.S.A.

Website address: www.lernerbooks.com

Library of Congress Cataloging-in-Publication Data

Doeden, Matt.
    Stay fit! : how you can get in shape / by Matt Doeden ; illustrated by Jack Desrocher ; Consultant: Sonja Green
      p. cm. — (Health Zone)
    Includes bibliographical references and index.
    ISBN 978–0–8225–7553–5 (lib. bdg. : alk. paper)
    1. Physical fitness—Juvenile literature. 2. Exercise—Juvenile literature. I. Desrocher, Jack, ill. II. Green, Sonja. III. Title.
RA781.D565 2009
613.7—dc22
                                                2007042163

Manufactured in the United States of America
1 2 3 4 5 6 — BP — 14 13 12 11 10 09

Table of Contents

Chris was breathing hard.

His legs felt like rubber.

He had been running back and forth across the soccer field for nearly an hour. **With less than one minute left in the game, his Panthers were beating the Mavericks 2–1.**

One of the opposing players kicked the ball toward Chris. It sailed through the air and bounced about 20 feet (6 meters) away. The Mavericks' striker was running hard after the ball. Chris realized that he couldn't get to it first, and he was the only defender between the Panthers' goal and the ball. So he stayed back to wait for the striker's charge.

Chris's opponent dribbled the ball forward. Chris moved to block him. Then the striker kicked the ball past Chris and darted toward the goal. The striker was quicker than Chris. But Chris noticed that he seemed sluggish after sprinting down the field. Chris still had enough energy left to chase after the striker and keep himself between the goal and the ball. By the time the striker passed the ball to a teammate, it was too late. More Panther defenders had run down the field to help Chris.

Someone blocked the Maverick player. He lost control of the ball. It bounced slowly toward Chris. *Chris took a big step and booted it as hard as he could toward the other end of the field.* Time ran out before the Mavericks could mount another attack on the Panthers' goal.

Chris stopped and bent over with his hands on his knees. He was tired, but he felt good about himself. He was physically fit enough to help his team win the game. After a couple of deep breaths, Chris ran over to join his cheering friends on the sidelines.

Suddenly, he didn't feel so tired anymore.

Chapter 1

WHAT IS Physical Fitness?

Physical fitness

is not about how far you can throw a ball or whether you look like a model.

You don't have to be the strongest or the fastest kid at school to be fit. Fitness is a measure of health. Being fit means being active and healthy.

Physical fitness is made up of eleven parts.

Six of the parts are skill related. **The other five are health related.** The parts that are related to skill help you to perform activities that require specific abilities. They help you to do well in things like sports or dance. The parts that are related to health help you to have a healthy body. *Let's take a look at the different parts of physical fitness.*

These parts of **physical fitness** are *skill* related.

 Agility. Agility is the ability to control your body movements. Agile people can quickly change directions to chase after a ball. **They can get out of the way if something falls in front of them.** Wrestlers and divers need to be agile to succeed in their sports.

 Balance. Balance is the ability to keep control of your body while moving. You need to have balance to ride a bike or a snowboard. Good balance also helps gymnasts and ice-skaters perform well.

3 **Coordination.** This is the ability to use your senses and body together. People with good coordination are good at games like baseball, golf, and tennis. They can see where a ball is going and move to catch or hit it.

Power. Power is a combination of speed and strength. **It is the ability to quickly use force.** Weight lifters and high jumpers need this skill. It helps sprinters and shot-putters too.

5 Reaction time. Reaction time is the amount of time it takes you to react to something. Having good reaction time allows you to quickly respond to situations. Infielders in baseball need to have good reaction time. They need to react quickly to catch line drives.

6 Speed. Speed has to do with how quickly you can move. But it's about more than just how fast you can run. **It's also about how fast you can throw a ball or swing a tennis racket.** It's important in all kinds of sports, from football to track to hockey.

AMAZING
Athletic feats

Baseball pitcher Joel Zumaya has had his fastball clocked at 103 miles (165 kilometers) per hour.

Male long-distance runner Haile Gebrselassie of Ethiopia ran the Berlin Marathon (more than 26 mi., or 41 km) in a record 2 hours, 4 minutes, and 26 seconds. The female record belongs to Paula Radcliffe of Great Britain. She ran the London Marathon (also more than 26 miles) in 2 hours, 15 minutes, and 25 seconds.

In the 2004 Summer Olympics, Udomporn Polsak of Thailand won gold by lifting 275 pounds (124 kilograms) over her head. Polsak herself weighed only about 115 pounds (52 kg)!

Everyone has different fitness levels in each of the skill-related areas. Some of us have a lot of power but may lack coordination. Others can easily walk across a balance beam but may not have a lot of speed. But through practice and training, anyone can improve in any skill-related area.

You may think that all athletes are good examples of physically fit people. But that isn't always true. A weight lifter could be out of breath after exercising for just a little while. A marathon runner might not be very strong. Some professional baseball players are overweight. And some football players aren't very flexible. Being fit is about many combined factors.

Good health does not come from skill-related physical fitness alone. It takes more than being good at sports to be healthy. And people who are bad at sports can be physically fit. Good health comes in part from doing health-related physical fitness activities.

These parts of **physical fitness** are *health* related.

1 **Cardiovascular fitness.** Cardiovascular fitness is a measure of how well your heart and blood vessels work. Cardiovascular fitness allows you to be active for long periods of time. It requires a strong heart and lungs and clean, unclogged blood vessels. If you have good cardiovascular fitness, you don't get tired just running around and playing with friends. Your heart provides your body with the oxygen it needs to keep going.

DID YOU KNOW?
Your cardiovascular system includes your heart and blood vessels.

2 **Flexibility.** Flexibility has to do with joint and muscle movement. Flexible people have no trouble moving their joints or their muscles. Their muscles are long and limber enough to allow their joints to move freely. **They can easily bend down to pick up a coin off the ground or reach up to grab a jar off a shelf.**

Muscular endurance. This is the ability to do something over and over again without tiring. You need muscular endurance to pedal a bike or play the drums. Shoveling snow and rowing a boat also require muscular endurance.

That's a Lot of Muscle!

If all your muscles pulled together, they could move about 25 tons (22 metric tons).

4 **Strength.** Strength is about how much weight you can lift or move. **If you have good strength, you can carry a backpack loaded with books or open a heavy door with little effort.**

5 **Body makeup.** Your body makeup has to do with what percentage of your body weight is made up of fat. For example, if you weigh 100 pounds (45 kg) and have 20 pounds (9 kg) of fat, your body fat is 20 percent. Maintaining a healthy level of body fat will help you avoid injuries and illnesses.

Healthful Body Fat

Healthful body fat percentages can vary based on age and whether you are male or female. But body fat percentages between about 18.5 and 24.9 are considered healthful for most people.

Just as some skill-related areas of fitness will come more easily to you than others, you'll have different strengths and weaknesses when it comes to health-related fitness. But by performing different exercises and activities, you can improve your fitness level in each area.

People often complain about exercising. They find excuses not to do it. But fitness isn't just about exercising. It's about doing physical activity, whether playing sports at school or dancing at a party. Even daily activities like walking your dog or biking to a friend's house will help improve your health.

Simply enjoying an active life will lead to better physical fitness.

Chapter 2

BENEFITS OF Physical Fitness

Why be active? Why worry about physical fitness?

For one thing, being healthy and being physically fit are closely related. If you are fit, your heart, lungs, and other organs will work more efficiently. For another thing, being out of shape can lead to health problems. **Type 2 diabetes, high blood pressure, and obesity (the condition of being very overweight) are all related to inactivity.** Being active can prevent or improve these conditions.

To understand how being inactive can affect your body, think about what happens if you break your right arm. A doctor puts a cast on the arm. You may have to wear it for weeks. Meanwhile, the muscles under the cast aren't moving. They're not getting any activity. When the doctor finally removes the cast, your right arm is slightly smaller than your left arm.

The muscles in the arm that was broken have started to waste away. This is called atrophy. Atrophy can happen when muscles don't get enough exercise. Muscles that have atrophied become less flexible. They're also easily injured. Your body will react in much the same way if you are inactive. **Fitness trainers often use the expression "use it or lose it."** And it's true! **To keep a healthy body, you have to actively use it.**

When being active, it's a good idea to keep the health-related areas of fitness in mind. These areas are especially important to anyone who wants to lead an active life. They will help you to stay strong and healthy during physical activity.

Cardiovascular fitness

Cardiovascular fitness is one of the most important areas of health-related physical fitness. It's closely related to disease prevention. It's also closely tied to your overall health. That's because cardiovascular fitness helps your body work more efficiently. As a result, you'll use less energy climbing stairs or doing other simple activities.

During long, tough periods of physical activity, your muscles aren't the only part of you getting a workout. So do your heart and lungs. (Your heart, in fact, is really just a big muscle.) When these organs are exercised, they get stronger. They become more efficient too. This means your heart can pump more blood with each beat. And your lungs can take in more air with each breath.

Did You Know?

Cardiovascular diseases are the leading cause of death in the United States. More than 60 percent of all deaths in the nation are caused by cardiovascular diseases. Many of these are the result of poor physical fitness.

Activity also helps your body make more blood. Blood contains red blood cells. These cells carry oxygen from your lungs to your muscles. Your muscles use this oxygen to create energy. In turn, you have more energy for sports or other activities.

Most people's hearts beat about seventy to eighty times a minute while resting. The resting heartbeat of a very fit person is lower. A fit person's heart might beat as few as fifty times per minute. A healthy heart can pump more blood with each beat. This means that the heart doesn't have to work as much. Consequently, the fit person has more energy.

Laid end to end, your blood vessels would measure 60,000 miles (97,000 km) long.

Another benefit to cardiovascular fitness is that your body will create more capillaries (small blood vessels) around your muscles. The increased number of capillaries helps supply your muscles with more oxygen. They're better equipped to run, dance, and play. **Jogging**, **swimming**, and **biking** are all examples of activities that can improve your cardiovascular fitness.

Creating Energy

Red blood cells pick up oxygen that you breathe into your lungs. These blood cells then travel throughout your body, delivering oxygen to your muscles and organs. As the oxygen mixes with glucose (a sugar) in your muscles, a chemical reaction called cellular respiration takes place. The reaction allows your muscles to create energy.

flexibility

Your muscles and joints need good flexibility to move freely. If you exercise your muscles without also stretching them out, they become tight and stiff. **Stiff muscles make it difficult to bend, twist, and reach for things.**

Athletes such as soccer players and football players have strong legs. But these athletes often injure their hamstrings or calf muscles during games. **Many muscle injuries can be prevented by having good flexibility. If your muscles and joints are able to move freely, you are less likely to strain or injure them while playing hard.** If you fall or bend a joint at an odd angle, you're less likely to suffer an injury if you're flexible. Some exercises, like toe touches, help increase flexibility.

Muscular Endurance

Endurance keeps your muscles in shape. *You gain endurance by performing a physical exercise over and over.* Activities like push-ups and curl-ups can build endurance. One benefit to increasing your muscular endurance is that your muscle cells develop more mitochondria. Mitochondria are small parts of cells. They create energy. The more mitochondria your muscle cells have, the more easily they can create energy when you need it. With good muscular endurance, you can do things longer and won't get cramps as quickly.

Muscular endurance helps you in other ways too. It allows you to play and work harder and longer without tiring. Another benefit is that you will have better posture and fewer back problems.

Joints

Joints are the spots where bones meet. Inside joints is a tough white tissue called cartilage. It keeps the bones from rubbing together. Fluid fills any empty space between the bones and cartilage. This fluid works like oil to lubricate the joints so they can move freely.

Strength

Skeletal muscles connect your bones and allow you to move. Like all muscles, they are made of fibers. When you work your skeletal muscles by lifting things or exercising, the fibers grow thicker. You become stronger. The thicker muscle fibers help you to more easily lift weight.

Strong muscles help you in work and play. You can swing a hammer harder or hit a ball farther. Having strong muscles also allows you to use less energy during daily activities, such as walking to school or doing chores at home. A strong body doesn't need to put out as much effort, so you'll have more energy to do the things you enjoy.

Strong muscles help to prevent injuries too. They provide support to your joints. The ligaments and tendons surrounding your joints also get stronger as your strength increases.

Body Makeup

The makeup of your body is important to your health. **If too much of your body weight is made up of fat, you will have health problems.** Your body will be

strained from carrying the extra weight. You will become tired more easily. Your cardiovascular health may also be harmed. Your heart will have to work extra hard to pump blood through your body.

Having too little fat isn't healthy either. If you have too little fat, you may be more prone to injuries during physical activities. You may be weak and have little energy. Your body might not work as it should.

Many people have the wrong amount of body fat. Having too much fat is more common than having too little. Excess body fat is a leading cause for developing certain diseases. One such disease is type 2 diabetes. This disease can damage blood vessels, the heart, kidneys, and eyes. It can even lead to death. Type 2 diabetes was once a disease that struck mainly inactive adults. But in recent years, as more kids have become overweight, it has become more common among children. Exercise and a healthful diet are the best ways to prevent it.

Many other issues are caused by having extra body fat. Joint pain and high blood pressure are some examples. Sleep apnea is another. This condition causes a temporary stoppage of breathing during sleep. Adults and children who suffer from sleep apnea often have restless nights. Restless nights can lead to fatigue (extreme tiredness), poor concentration, and poor growth.

The Importance of Sleep

Most young people need about ten hours of sleep each night. Sleep gives your body energy and mental clarity. It also allows your body to rest and recover from injuries. It is healthiest to go to sleep at the same time every night and get up at the same time every morning.

Other Benefits to Physical Fitness

Being physically fit has many benefits. If you're fit, you are less likely to become tired. **You will sleep better. You are also less likely to experience stress.** That's because exercise releases special chemicals in your brain. The chemicals help you to stay calm and happy.

Being fit also allows you to rise to the occasion in emergencies. You'll be able to run for help when someone is in need. You'll have the strength to pull someone to safety.

Having good physical fitness helps prevent many health problems.·············⋮

Physical fitness will strengthen your body against illnesses like colds and flus. It will even help protect you against major diseases. People who are fit are less likely to suffer from heart disease. And research has shown that people who are physically active are less likely to get certain types of cancer.

Physical fitness simply leads to a better, happier life.

Not only will you be more physically fit, but you will also feel better and look better. You will be healthier and have more energy. Having more energy allows you to be more active. This, in turn, leads to better fitness and improved health. This pattern is known as the physical fitness cycle. If you continue the cycle throughout your life, you will lead a longer, healthier one.

DID YOU KNOW?
In the United States,
about 250,000 people
die prematurely each year
because they were not
physically fit.

The Physical Fitness Cycle

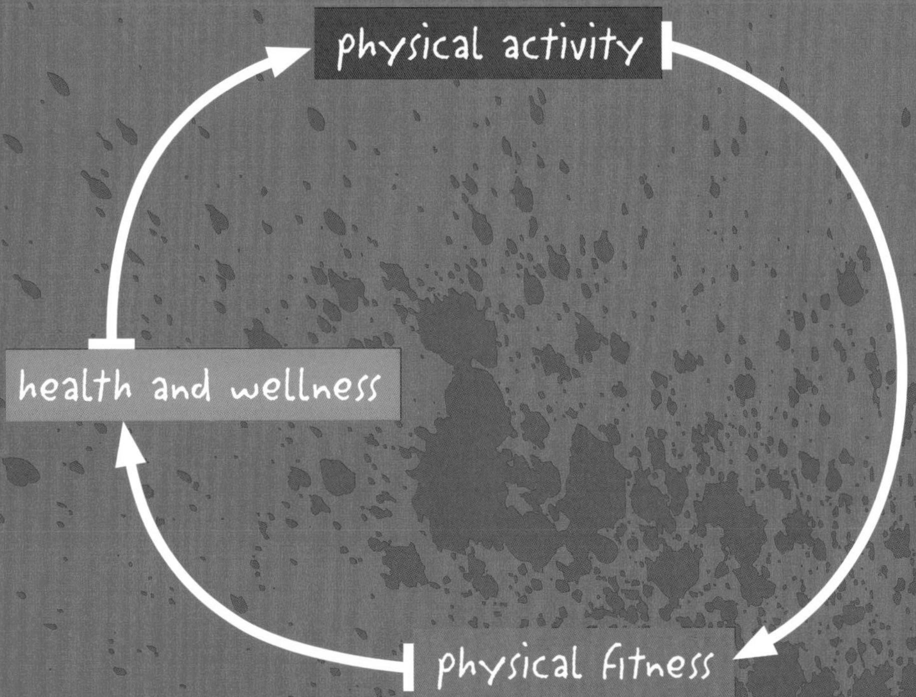

physical activity

physical fitness

health and wellness

Chapter 3

Fueling
YOUR BODY

You can't drive a car without gas.

Your radio won't blare music without batteries.

You can't play your favorite video game if it's not plugged in.

Like these machines, your body needs fuel, or energy, to work.

Food provides your body with the energy it needs. Food contains healthful substances called nutrients. Nutrients help your body function. They allow you to be physically active. For this reason, physical fitness and nutrition go hand in hand. After all, food provides the energy you need to be active. And if you don't eat the right types of foods, your body won't work properly.

Six main kinds of nutrients appear in food. Three of these nutrients—carbohydrates, fats, and proteins—provide your body with energy. The other three—minerals, vitamins, and water—do not provide energy. But they're still important sources of fuel for your body.

Breakfast

Have you ever heard anyone say that breakfast is the most important meal of the day? It's true. Breakfast resupplies your body with the energy it used up since your last meal—

usually about twelve hours earlier! Breakfast gives you energy to do better in school. It also helps you control your body fat. If you skip breakfast, you're more likely to overeat at your next meal.

Types of Nutrients

Carbohydrates.

Carbohydrates are sugars and starches found in foods. People often call them carbs for short. Your body breaks down carbs into glucose. Glucose is your body's main source of energy.

Your body gets two types of carbohydrates: complex and simple. Complex carbs come mainly from grains and vegetables. They are rich with nutrients. Some complex carbs are better than others. But most of the carbs you eat should be complex carbs.

Simple carbs can be found in candy, soft drinks, and some fruits. They contain many calories. (Calories are a measurement of the amount of energy a food gives you.) Simple carbs also tend to have a lower nutritional value than complex carbs do.

Fats.

Fats are a nutrient found in animal products, nuts, and vegetable oils. They help repair and maintain your body. Food contains three main types of fats: saturated, unsaturated, and trans fats. Saturated fats come from foods such as butter and meat. Most doctors recommend limiting the amount of saturated fats you eat. Unsaturated fats come from foods such as plants and fish. These are healthful fats that your body needs. Trans fats are artificial fats. They are found in some baked goods. Trans fats are a type of unsaturated fat. But they are not healthful. Most doctors recommend avoiding them.

Proteins.

Proteins help build body tissue and maintain your cells. They are found in meat, eggs, and milk. Some grains, nuts, and beans also contain proteins.

Minerals. Minerals control some of your cells' functions. For example, the mineral potassium balances the fluids in your cells. It also maintains nerve, muscle, and heart function. Iron helps oxygen move from red blood cells to other cells. It's important for brain development and immune system functioning too. In total, your body needs twenty-five different minerals.

Vitamins. Vitamins help your body grow and repair cells. They provide a wide range of benefits. For instance, vitamin B_2 breaks down carbohydrates and proteins. Meanwhile, niacin helps release the energy from carbohydrates and proteins. Vitamin C helps your body heal. Your body needs more than one dozen types of vitamins.

Water.

Water is very important for your body. It's the grease that lubricates your body's mechanics. Water keeps the chemical reactions in your body going. It carries all the other nutrients to cells. It also carries waste away from cells. It helps control your body temperature too. More than half your body weight is actually made up of water.

Did You Know?

The color of your urine can tell you if you're drinking enough water. Dark yellow urine means you're dehydrated. If your urine is nearly clear, you have enough water in your body.

Consuming Nutrients Wisely

A fit person must carefully think about the nutrients that he or she is taking in. **It's important to make sure that you're getting the right amounts—and the right types—of nutrients.** For example, you don't want to overdo saturated fats. That can be hard on your heart. And you don't want to take in too many simple carbs either. The simple carbs in a candy bar or a can of soda may give you a quick burst of energy. But it won't last. Since simple carbs often lack nutritional value, they can leave you feeling more tired and hungry than you were before.

How Much Soda Do You Drink?

The calories from drinking one can of regular soda a day for a whole year will add up to about 15 pounds (6 kg) of fat.

The best way to get your nutrients is by eating a diet rich in a variety of fresh, healthful foods. This kind of diet will provide you with all the nutrients you need. That doesn't mean you can't eat a burger and fries once in a while. Just remember that junk foods tend to have a lot of simple carbs. They trick your body into thinking it's been fed when it's really craving more nutritional foods. Healthy foods are what your body requires to maintain a healthful level of physical fitness.

Chapter 4

HOW Fit ARE YOU?

A physically fit person can perform most daily activities without getting tired.

Raking the yard, walking up a flight of stairs, or biking to the store shouldn't tire a fit person.

If you're fit, you can go to school, come home and do chores, and still have energy to play with friends.

If, when you get home, you're too tired to play or help around the house, you may not be physically fit. *(Or you may need to get more sleep.)*

One way to better understand how fit you are is through self-assessment. Test yourself in each of the five health-related areas of fitness. Then you'll know which areas are your strong points and which you may want to work on a little.

Cardiovascular Fitness Test

One good way to test your cardiovascular fitness is by checking your heart rate after walking up and down a flight of stairs. Here's how. First, check your resting heart rate. Place two fingers against your wrist, just below your palm, to find your pulse. Then count the beats over fifteen seconds. Multiply this number by four. This final number is your resting heart rate. Next, time yourself walking up and down steps for three minutes. Keep a steady—but not slow—pace. When the three minutes are up, are you breathing harder? Check your heart rate. Is it higher? Wait one full minute and check again. Is your heart rate still faster than it usually is? If so, you probably could improve your cardiovascular fitness.

Alternatives to Running

Lots of people think of running when they picture a cardiovascular workout. And for some people, running is a great way to build a healthy heart. But what if running just isn't for you? Never fear! There are lots of great cardiovascular activities for you to try. Here are just a few.

Dancing

Skipping or jumping rope

In-line skating. (Don't forget your knee and elbow pads. And make sure to strap on that helmet!)

Walking. (That's right. Walking! Going for a walk can be a great way to build your cardiovascular fitness. Just make sure you're walking fast enough to raise your heart rate a little.)

flexibility Test

Next try testing your flexibility. You can do this by performing the V-sit reach. What's the V-sit reach? It's a test set up by the President's Council on Physical Fitness and Sports. This group has developed lots of tests that kids can try to check their fitness levels. To do the V-sit reach, use masking tape to make a line about 2 feet (0.6 m) long across the floor. This will be the baseline. Then make another line that runs perpendicular and through the middle of the baseline. This second line is the measuring line. Where the two lines meet is zero. From zero, make a mark every inch (2.5 centimeters) in both directions along the measuring line.

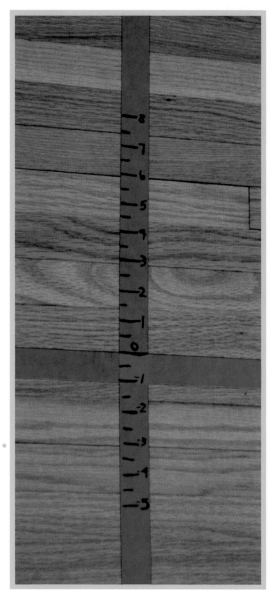

When you're done, sit down on the measuring line. . . . .
Place the heels of your feet on the baseline.
They should be about 8 to 12 inches (20 to 30 cm) apart. Next, place your hands on the measuring line, palms down. Extend your arms slowly along the line toward the zero. Take three practice tries. On the fourth try, slowly reach as far as you can. Count how many inch or centimeter marks away from the zero you were.

If you're a boy around the age of twelve, you should be able to reach about one inch (2.5 cm) beyond the zero.

A twelve-year-old girl should be able to reach about 3.5 inches (8.9 cm) beyond the zero.

Boys and girls who can reach farther are extremely flexible. Those who can't quite reach that far shouldn't worry. It just means they may want to practice the V-sit reach to develop their flexibility.

Muscular Endurance and Strength Test

Your strength and muscular endurance are closely related. You can test them at the same time by performing two exercises. **First, count the number of curl-ups you can do. Lie on your back with knees flexed and your feet** ...... **about 12 inches (30 cm) from your buttocks.** Cross your arms, placing your left hand on your right shoulder and your right hand on your left shoulder. Have someone hold your feet. When you're ready, lift your trunk, curling up so that your elbows touch your thighs. Count how many times you can do this in a minute.

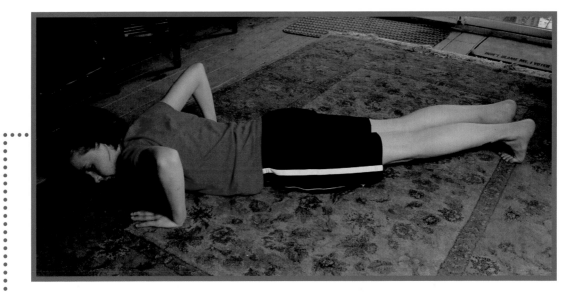

Next, test how many push-ups you can do. Lie flat on the floor, on your chest, with your hands under your shoulders. Your palms should be touching the floor. Using your toes to support your feet, push your body off the ground by straightening your arms. Be sure not to bend your back or knees. Pause for a moment. Then lower your body until your chest touches the floor. Do one push-up every three seconds for as long as you can, counting as you go. Stop when you can no longer keep up the pace of one push-up every three seconds.

Boys around the age of twelve should be able to do about forty curl-ups and eighteen push-ups.

Girls around the age of twelve should be able to do about thirty-five curl-ups and ten push-ups.

If you can hit these targets, you probably have good muscular endurance and strength. If you can do more, your strength and endurance are probably excellent! If you can't quite hit these targets, it's no reason to worry. Try doing a few curl-ups and push-ups every day to build your muscles. As your strength and endurance improve, add a few more curl-ups and push-ups to your routine. *After a few months, you may find that you're easily hitting the targets.*

Body Fat Test

The makeup of your body can also tell you a lot about your fitness. It's a good idea to know how much of your body weight is made up of fat. One measurement of body fat is called **body mass index**, or **BMI**. It's calculated through a special formula. First you multiply your weight in pounds by 703. Then you divide by your height in inches. Finally, you divide again by your height in inches. Here's an equation for example:

100 pounds x 703 = 70,300 ÷ 58 = 1212 ÷ 58 = 21

If your body mass index is in the healthy range, you probably have a healthful percentage of body fat.

To check your **BMI**, you'll need to know your height and weight. So pull out a tape measure and step on a scale. A friend can help you do the measuring. Once you know your height and weight, log onto this site from the Centers for Disease Control and Prevention: http://apps.nccd.cdc.gov/dnpabmi/Calculator.aspx. It has a handy **BMI calculator** you can use. It can help you to easily and accurately determine your **BMI**.

BMI

BMI can be a good way to measure your body fat. But the BMI measurement isn't perfect. Very muscular people may have high BMIs—even if they don't have much body fat. That's because BMI can't always tell the difference between muscle and fat.

It's Not a COMPETITION

Keep in mind that self-assessment *is not a competition.* It doesn't mean you're unfit if your friend can reach much farther in the V-sit test. And it doesn't mean you're fit if you can do more push-ups than someone else. Self-assessment is about understanding your level of physical fitness. Once you know how fit you are in each area of health-related physical fitness, you can work to improve your fitness levels.

Chapter 5

ALL ABOUT Exercise

EXERCISE is any activity that you do with the goal of improving your fitness.

You can try many different exercises.
Some exercises are aerobic. These exercises raise your heart and breathing rates. Others focus on strength training. These exercises build your muscles. Whatever kind of exercise you do, it's important to pick activities that you enjoy. This will ensure that you'll stick with your workout. It will also guarantee that you'll have fun!

Most doctors recommend a minimum of sixty minutes of exercise every day. But remember to take it easy, especially at first. Exercising too much can lead to injuries and can damage your growing body. You need to start with a level of exercise that is comfortable for you. Then you can slowly build up to more vigorous workouts. You also need to make sure to perform all exercises properly. This will help you get the most out of your workout.

Getting advice on your exercise program is a good idea. Try talking to a phy ed teacher or a doctor. They can teach you how to do exercises correctly so that you don't hurt yourself. They can also show you which exercises will best help you to achieve your goals.

Stretching and Warming Up

Warming up is an important part of any safe workout.
It prepares your body for physical activity. Warming up your muscles will allow them to stretch and relax more easily. You will also be less likely to strain or injure your muscles.

S t r e t c h i n g is a great way to warm up before a workout. S t r e t c h i n g your muscles also helps improve your flexibility. But remember to do it carefully. Extend slowly and hold a stretch position. Relax between stretches. You should stretch until your muscles feel tight. If it becomes painful, then you're stretching too far. You should never bounce or jerk while s t r e t c h i n g . You could pull or strain a muscle.

Yoga

Yoga is a form of exercise that involves holding certain poses and positions. It increases balance. Yoga is a great way to improve flexibility.

It's best to stretch out all your muscles before you begin exercising. To stretch your back, you can perform a back twist. Stand, looking forward, with your knees slightly bent and your hands hanging at your sides. Slowly twist to your right until you are looking directly behind you. Hold this position for a few seconds. Then slowly twist all the way to the left until you are looking behind you. *Do ten to fifteen twists.*

To stretch your legs, you can perform the V-sit reach. Remember the V-sit reach? You read about this exercise in chapter 4. It involves sitting on the floor with your legs about 8 to 12 inches apart (20 to 30 cm apart). You then place your hands between your knees, palms down, and extend your arms forward slowly. When you perform the V-sit reach this time, try holding the position for a few seconds each time you reach forward. Then relax. *Repeat the V-sit reach ten to fifteen times.*

A good exercise to stretch your arms is the upper arm stretch. Keeping your elbow straight, hold your right arm out straight in front of you. Then with your left hand, grab the outside of your right elbow. Slowly pull your arm toward the front of your body until you feel a gentle stretch. Hold it for a few seconds. Then switch to your left arm. *Repeat several times.*

Warm-Ups for Athletes

If you play sports, it's always smart to
stretch before you hit the field or court.
But you may want to try some other warm-
up movements too. In addition to stretching,
try performing movements that are similar
to the activity you'll be doing. For example,
if you're going to be playing tennis, you can
warm up by taking some practice swings and
serves. If you're
going to be playing
softball, play catch
before the game.
This type of warm-
up can help to get
your muscles going.
It can help you to
play hard without
getting hurt.

Aerobic Fitness

Once your muscles are warmed up, you're ready to exercise. **Aerobic exercises are a good place to start. These exercises force your body to use a lot of oxygen.** They work your cardiovascular system. Aerobic exercises cause your heart to beat faster and your muscles to need more oxygen to create energy. They burn lots of calories. This helps you lose body fat.

Losing Weight

Many people turn to special diets in hopes of losing weight. But the best way to shed pounds is through aerobic exercise and sensible eating. Much of the weight you lose while on a weight-loss diet is water, not body fat. So as soon as you go off the diet, you gain the weight back. Exercise burns off body fat and builds muscles. And by eating healthfully, you can make sure the weight doesn't come back.

Some examples of aerobic exercise are biking, running, and swimming**. You can also try ice-skating** or **cross-country skiing**. If skating and skiing aren't available where you live, check out **martial arts**. Karate and **aerobic kick boxing** are some examples. **Aerobic dance** is another popular form of exercise. It combines aerobic movements and dance steps. Aerobic dance routines are performed to music. And you can do aerobic dance to any type of music, whether you enjoy jazz, hip-hop, or rock.

No matter what type of aerobic exercise you do, the important thing is to elevate your heart rate while exercising. The best way to do this is through ongoing activity. This is why doctors recommend at least sixty minutes of physical activity a day. Prolonged activity improves your overall fitness.

Zumba

Zumba is a type of aerobic dance that's performed to Latin music. It uses moves from traditional dances, such the merengue, salsa, and mambo. Zumba is designed to be a fun activity. But it has all the benefits of other aerobic exercises. If you don't like sports or going to the gym, it's a great alternative.

Strength Training

Another type of exercise is strength training. **Progressive resistance exercises (PREs)** are an important part of strength training. They're a great way to build your muscles and gain muscular endurance. **PREs** involve gradually—or progressively—increasing the amount of work your muscles perform. You can use your own body weight to do **PREs**.

Push-ups and curl-ups use your own body weight as resistance. Each push-up or curl-up you do is called a repetition, or rep. When you exercise, try to do a certain number of reps. For example, you could start with ten push-ups. When you complete the ten push-ups, that is one set.

Once you're able to complete one set of push-ups, you are ready to add a second set to your workout. Do one set, rest for a minute, and then do a second set. When you're able to reach your goal on the second set, add a third set. Once you can reach your goal for three sets, increase the number of reps you do. This is how you progressively increase resistance. **Repetition is what builds muscle. It also improves muscle endurance.**

Cool Down

Just as it's important to warm up muscles before exercising, it's important to cool them down afterward. A cool-down period will prevent your muscles from becoming stiff and sore. It will help you to recover from physical activity.

To cool down your heart, do an aerobic activity, such as walking or jogging, at a slower pace. To cool down other muscles, try some stretches. *Not only will stretches keep your muscles from getting sore—they'll also help you build your flexibility*. Since your muscles will be warm and loose from exercising, you'll be able to stretch them further than normal.

Disc Golf

Disc golf is a sport that has been around for many years. Disc golfers use discs (like Frisbees) to hit a target. They try to reach a number of targets on a course. They stretch and exercise their arms as they throw discs at different targets. They also do a lot of walking—sometimes up hills, down valleys, and through groves of trees. Anyone can play disc golf. You don't have to join a team to get in on the fun. Many communities have courses where you can play for free.

In the end, being healthy and physically fit is all about the lifestyle you choose.

You can watch TV or play a pick-up game with friends.

You can get a ride everywhere you go, or you can walk or ride a bike.

You don't need to go to a gym or play sports to stay fit. You just need to be physically active. **The key to physical fitness is finding activities that you enjoy, whether it's in-line skating, playing baseball with the neighbors, or walking your dog. Whatever activity you choose, make sure to stay active for at least sixty minutes every day.**

And don't forget to have fun!

Quiz

Now that you've read all about physical fitness, try this fun quiz to see how much you know. Please record your answers on a separate sheet of paper. (Answers appear near the bottom of page 57.)

1. **Which of the following statements about skill-related physical fitness is true?**
   a. It can help you to do well in sports.
   b. It's made up of five parts.
   c. It's only for jocks.
   d. Both a and b

2. **Which of the following is an important area of health-related physical fitness?**
   a. Agility
   b. Power
   c. Flexibility
   d. Penmanship

3. **What does it mean if a muscle has started to atrophy?**
   a. It means that the muscle is getting stronger.
   b. It means that the muscle has started to waste away.
   c. It means that the muscle needs more rest.
   d. It means that the muscle has lots of muscle fibers.

4. **The best way to gain muscular endurance is to:**
   a. Do stretching exercises
   b. Perform a physical exercise over and over
   c. Cut calories
   d. Watch pro wrestling

5. **Which of the following conditions can result from having too much body fat?**
   a. Type 2 diabetes
   b. High blood pressure
   c. Sleep apnea
   d. All of the above

6. **Which test would be the best measure of your cardiovascular fitness?**

   a. A test that measured how far you could reach

   b. A test that measured how many curl-ups you could do in a minute

   c. A test that measured your heart rate after you walked up and down a flight of stairs

   d. A test that measured how long you could shop before you dropped

7. **What is the minimum amount of exercise that most doctors recommend?**

   a. Thirty minutes every day

   b. Sixty minutes every other day

   c. Sixty minutes every day

   d. Doctors don't recommend any exercise.

8. **How is BMI used?**

   a. To give a rough measurement of how large your muscles are

   b. To give a rough measurement of how much body fat you have

   c. To give a rough measurement of your flexibility

   d. To give a rough measurement of your cardiovascular fitness

9. **What is the purpose of performing a warm-up?**

   a. To prepare your body for physical activity

   b. To help you recover from physical activity

   c. To burn calories

   d. To make you sweat

10. **Physical activity leads to:**

    a. Better physical fitness

    b. Having more energy

    c. Better health

    d. All of the above

My Physical Activity Log

Keeping a physical activity log can be a great way to measure your fitness levels. Here's how you can start a fitness log of your own:

First, find a notebook and a pencil. Mark the date on the top of the first page of your notebook. Then, using the exercises in chapter 4, test your levels of physical fitness. Perform each exercise, and record your results next to the exercise.

Once you know your results, try to keep track of all the activities you do for a month—whether it's sitting in class, playing video games, biking to a friend's, or exercising. Write down how much time you spend on each of the activities.

After the month is over, try the fitness activities in chapter 4 again. Write the date at the top of the page, and mark down all your results.

Check your first set of results against your second set. Did they improve? No matter what your answer is, look back over your log of activities and put a star by any that you would consider "physical" activities.

If you have lots of stars but didn't improve your results, think of other activities that might help you to become more fit. Maybe you could play a game of basketball instead of playing catch or bike around the neighborhood instead of walking. If you don't have many stars, take a look at your activities and decide which ones you could replace with physical activities.

Here's a sample of a physical activity log to help you get started with your own fitness record keeping.

PHYSICAL ACTIVITY LOG
October 23

FITNESS TESTS

Cardiovascular
Resting heart rate: 60 beats per minute
Heart rate after stair climb: 70 bpm
Heart rate one minute later: 60 bpm

Flexibility
V-sit reach: 3 inches (7 cm)

Muscular Endurance and Strength
Curl-ups: 35
Push-ups: 20

Body Fat
BMI: 19.5

ACTIVITIES THIS MONTH
Sitting in Class — 126 hours
Exercising — 15 hours
Dance Lessons — 5 hours
Watching TV — 25 hours
Playing Soccer with Friends — 7 hours
Doing Homework — 15 hours

Glossary

aerobic exercise: exercise that raises your heart and breathing rates

atrophy: the wasting away of a body part or tissue

body mass index (BMI): a rough measurement of body fat

calorie: a measurement of the amount of energy a food gives you

capillary: a small blood vessel

cardiovascular fitness: a measure of how well your heart and blood vessels work

glucose: a sugar. Glucose is your body's main source of energy.

joint: the spot where bones meet

mitochondria: small parts of cells. Mitochondria create energy.

nutrient: a healthful substance found in food

obesity: the condition of being very overweight

progressive resistance exercise (PRE): exercise that involves gradually increasing the amount of work your muscles perform

skeletal muscle: a muscle that connects your bones and allows you to move

sleep apnea: a condition that causes a temporary stoppage of breathing during sleep. Sleep apnea can be caused by having extra body fat.

strength training: exercise that builds your muscles

type 2 diabetes: a disease caused by a lack of the hormone insulin. Type 2 diabetes is often caused by being overweight.

Selected Bibliography

Corbin, Charles B., and Ruth Lindsey. *Fitness for Life*. Champaign, IL: Human Kinetics, 2007.

Ditson, Mary, Caesar Pacifici, and Lee White. *The Teenage Human Body's Operator's Manual*. Eugene, OR: Northwest Media, 1998.

Landy, Joanne, and Keith Burridge. *50 Simple Things You Can Do to Raise a Child Who Is Physically Fit*. New York: Macmillan, 1997.

Mazel, Judy, and John E. Monaco. *Slim & Fit Kids: Raising Healthy Children in a Fast-Food World*. Deerfield Beach, FL: Health Communications: 1999.

Nemours Foundation. *KidsHealth*. 2008. http://www.kidshealth .org (February 29, 2008).

President's Challenge. *Presidentschallenge.org*. N.d. http://www .presidentschallenge.org (February 29, 2008).

Schlosberg, Suzanne, and Liz Neporent. *Fitness for Dummies*. Foster City, CA: IDG Books, 1996.

Sharkey, Brian J. *Fitness & Health*. Champaign, IL: Human Kinetics, 2002.

USDA. *MyPyramid.gov*. N.d. http://www.mypyramid.gov (February 29, 2008).

Wnek, Barb. *Celebration Games: Physical Activities for Every Month*. Champaign, IL: Human Kinetics, 2006.

Doeden, Matt. *Eat Right!: How You Can Make Good Food Choices*. Minneapolis: Lerner Publications Company, 2009. Learn more about how nutrition paired with exercise can help you lead a healthful life.

Gray, Shirley W. *Exercising for Good Health*. Chanhassen, MN: Child's World, 2004. This simple guide helps students understand the important role physical fitness plays in being healthy.

It's My Life
http://pbskids.org/itsmylife
Visit this site to read up on a variety of health-related issues, including physical fitness and nutrition.

KidsHealth
http://www.kidshealth.org/kid
This site contains a wealth of information to help kids better understand their bodies.

MyPyramid
http://www.mypyramid.gov
This site from the USDA offers useful information on how to eat a healthful diet.

Rockwell, Lizzy. *The Busy Body Book: A Kid's Guide to Fitness*. New York: Crown Publishers, 2004. Rockwell provides a basic introduction to physical fitness as well as interesting facts on how the human body works.

Schwager, Tina, and Michele Schuerger. *The Right Moves: A Girl's Guide to Getting Fit and Feeling Good*. Minneapolis: Free Spirit, 1998. Schwager and Schuerger provide tips for girls on exercising, eating right, and maintaining a positive attitude.

Silverstein, Alvin, Virginia Silverstein, and Laura Silverstein Nunn. *Physical Fitness*. New York: Franklin Watts, 2002. Learn more about physical fitness and how you can achieve good health.

Index

Photo/Illustration Acknowledgments

The images in this book are used with the permission of: © Thomas Barwick/Digital Vision/Getty Images, p. 4; © Robert Glenn/ DK Stock/ Getty Images, p. 6; © Imagestate/Alamy, p. 7; © age fotostock/ SuperStock, pp. 11, 57 ; © Steve Satushek/Photographer's Choice/ Getty Images, p. 13 (bottom); © Chev Wilkenson/Stone/Getty Images, p. 15; © Brooke Slezak/Taxi/Getty Images, p. 16; © Russell Illig/ Photodisc/Getty Images, p. 17; © Ableimages/Riser/Getty Images, p. 20; © Erik Isakson/Rubberball Productions/Getty Images, pp. 21, 38; © iStockphoto.com/stockphoto4u, p. 22; © Michael Malyszko/Taxi/ Getty Images, p. 23; © Tetra Images/Getty Images, p. 24; © David Deas/DK Stock/Getty Images, p. 26; © Jose Luis Palaez Inc./Getty Images, p. 28; © Rubberball Productions/Getty Images, pp. 30, 31; © Comstock Images, p. 32 (top); © Artproem/Dreamstime.com, p. 32 (bottom); © MegapressAlamy, p. 33; © Blasius Erlinger/The Image Bank/Getty Images, p. 34 (top); © Fotoeye75/Dreamstime.com, p. 34 (bottom); © Alistair Berg/Taxi/Getty Images, p. 35; © Lori Adamski Peek/The Image Bank/Getty Images, p. 36; © Julie Caruso, pp. 40, 41 (both), 42, 43, 46, 49; © Leander Baerenz/Photonica/Getty Images, p. 47; © Pat Thielen/ Alamy, p. 50; © Nir Alon/Alamy, p. 51; © Todd Strand/Independent Picture Service, p. 52; © John Giustina/Iconica/ Getty Images, p. 53; © Ian Boddy/Photo Researchers, Inc., p. 56.

Front Cover: © Lori Adamski Peek/Getty Images.

About the Author

Matt Doeden is a freelance author and editor living in Minnesota. He's written and edited hundreds of children's books on topics ranging from genetic engineering to rock climbing to monster trucks.